Wild Predators!

Killer Cats

Heinemann
LIBRARY

Andrew Solway

www.heinemann.co.uk/library
Visit our website to find out more information about **Heinemann Library** books.

To order:
 Phone 44 (0) 1865 888066
 Send a fax to 44 (0) 1865 314091
Visit the Heinemann Bookshop at www.heinemann.co.uk/library to browse our catalogue and order online.

First published in Great Britain by
Heinemann Library, Halley Court, Jordan Hill,
Oxford OX2 8EJ, part of Harcourt Education.
Heinemann is a registered trademark of Harcourt
Education Ltd.

Editorial: Nancy Dickmann, Tanvi Rai and Sarah
Chappelow
Design: David Poole and Calcium
Illustrations: Geoff Ward
Picture Research: Maria Joannou and Catherine
Bevan
Production: Camilla Smith

Originated by Ambassador Litho Ltd.
Printed and bound in China by
South China Printing Company.
The paper used to print this book comes from
sustainable resources.

ISBN 0 431 19006 2
08 07 06 05
10 9 8 7 6 5 4 3 2 1

**British Library Cataloguing in Publication
Data**
Solway, Andrew
Killer Cats. – (Wild predators)
  599.7'73153
A full catalogue record for this book is available
from the British Library.

Acknowledgements
The Publishers would like to thank the following
for permission to reproduce photographs:
Ardea pp. **13 top** (Tom & Pat Leeson), **21** (Clem
Haagner), **31** (Clem Haagner), **43** (Ferraro Lebat);
Corbis pp. **14** (Roger De La Harpe/Gallo Images),
25 bottom, **28** (Tom Brakefield), **29** (Wayne
Bennett), **39** (Tom Brakefield), **41** (Galen Rowell);
FLPA pp. **6** (Michael Callan), **8** (Yossi Eshbol), **10**
(Philip Perry), **13 bottom** (Gerard Lacz), **16**
(Wendy Dennis), **17** (Gerard Lacz), **20** (P Davey),
23 (Albert Visage), **27** (Silvestris), **32** (Fritz
Polking), **37** (t Whittaker), **38** (Silvestris), **40**
(Fritz Polking), **42** (Mark Newman); Getty Images
pp. **25 top** (Photodisc), **32**; NHPA pp. **4** (Andy
Rouse), **5 top** (Joe Blossom), **5 bottom** (Martin
Harvey), **22** (Martin Harvey), **26** (Andy Rouse);
Oxford Scientific Films pp. **7 top** (Konrad
Wothe), **7 bottom** (Norbert Rosing), **9** (Eyal
Bartov), **11** (Partridge Films), **15** (Michael
Fogden), **18** (Daniel Cox), **19** (Marty Stouffer
Prods/AA), **33** (Brian Kenney), **34** (Daniel Cox),
35 top (Daniel Cox), **35 bottom** (Colin
Monteath), **36** (Alan & Sandy Carey).

Cover photograph of an African lion chasing
Kudu, panthera leo, Etosha National Park,
Namibia reproduced with permission of
HNPA/Martin Harvey.

The Publishers would like to thank Michael Bright
of the BBC Natural History Unit for his
assistance in the preparation of this book.

Every effort has been made to contact copyright
holders of any material reproduced in this book.
Any omissions will be rectified in subsequent
printings if notice is given to the Publishers.

Disclaimer

Contents

Any words appearing in the text in bold, **like this**, are explained in the Glossary.

Ultimate predators

Think of a **predator**. The first animal that comes into your mind will probably be a cat. You might think of a lion roaring, or a cheetah bounding across the grassland after a gazelle. You might think of a tiger pulling down a wild bull, or perhaps your own pet cat stalking a bird. Lions, tigers, cheetahs, and pet cats are part of the cat family – the Felidae. All of them are superb predators.

Designed for hunting

A cat's body is designed for hunting. Most cats do not have particularly long legs, but their flexible spine makes them agile and quick over the ground. A cat's jaw is short, and this gives it a very powerful bite. It has two pairs of dagger-like front teeth (the **canines**), which it can sink deep into its **prey**. A cat also has a second set of weapons – its razor-sharp, curved claws. It can use these to slash open its prey, or as grappling hooks to climb on to prey or to pull it down.

A cat has excellent senses for tracking down prey. Most cats hunt at night, so their eyesight is especially good when there is little light. Their eyes are large, and the **pupils** can open very wide to allow in as much light as possible. Cats also have sensitive hearing to listen for the sounds of prey moving. Long whiskers on either side of their **muzzle** help them to feel their way in confined spaces. Cats also have a much better sense of smell than humans, although they do not rely on their noses as much as dogs.

All cats except cheetahs can **retract** their claws to protect them and help keep them sharp. As well as acting as weapons, sharp claws help cats such as this jaguar to climb.

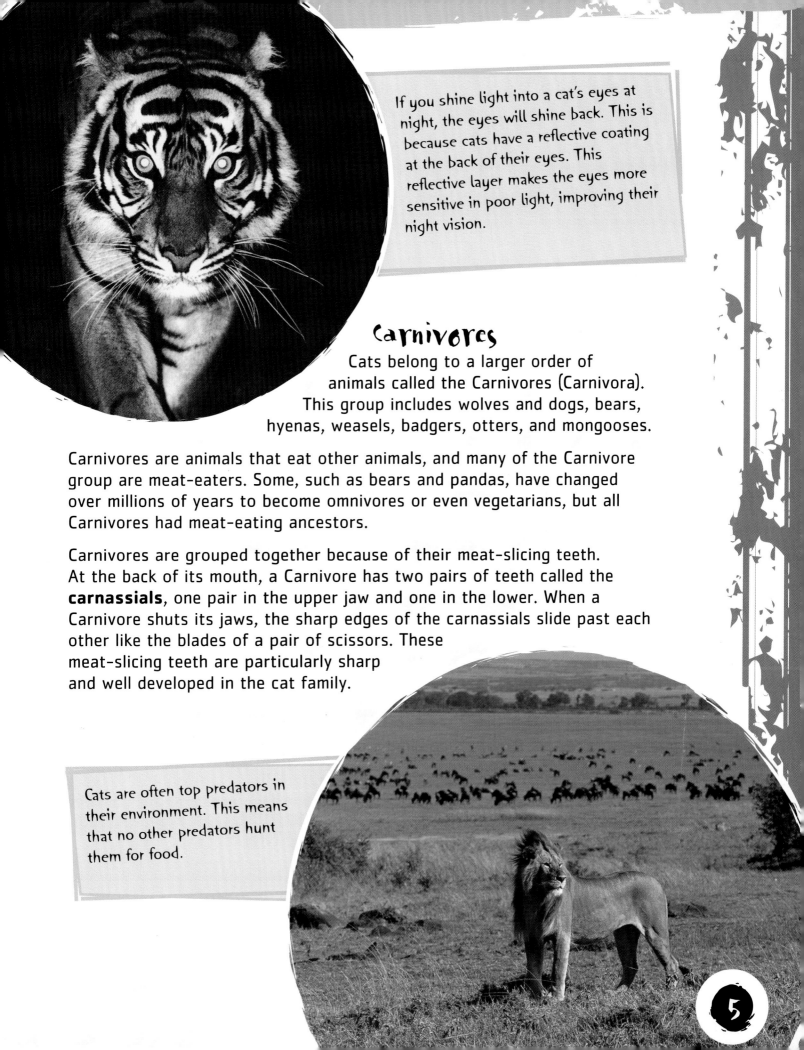

If you shine light into a cat's eyes at night, the eyes will shine back. This is because cats have a reflective coating at the back of their eyes. This reflective layer makes the eyes more sensitive in poor light, improving their night vision.

Carnivores

Cats belong to a larger order of animals called the Carnivores (Carnivora). This group includes wolves and dogs, bears, hyenas, weasels, badgers, otters, and mongooses.

Carnivores are animals that eat other animals, and many of the Carnivore group are meat-eaters. Some, such as bears and pandas, have changed over millions of years to become omnivores or even vegetarians, but all Carnivores had meat-eating ancestors.

Carnivores are grouped together because of their meat-slicing teeth. At the back of its mouth, a Carnivore has two pairs of teeth called the **carnassials**, one pair in the upper jaw and one in the lower. When a Carnivore shuts its jaws, the sharp edges of the carnassials slide past each other like the blades of a pair of scissors. These meat-slicing teeth are particularly sharp and well developed in the cat family.

Cats are often top predators in their environment. This means that no other predators hunt them for food.

Wildcat

A female wildcat with young kittens sits outside her den in western Scotland. She sits quietly, with just the tip of her tail twitching. The kittens are fascinated by her twitching tail. They slowly creep up on it, then, pounce suddenly. Often the mother whisks her tail away, but sometimes a kitten grabs the tail and gives it a good bite. This is the start of a kitten's hunting training.

Wildcats are small cats, with a body 50 to 80 centimetres (20 to 30 inches) long. They live in Europe, north Africa, and Asia. They prefer to live in open woodland, but they are also found in **conifer** forests, moorlands, and swamps.

Domestic cats

The ancient Egyptians first began keeping cats about 4000 years ago. The cats they kept were wildcats from Africa.

Stalk and pounce

Wolves and dogs are tireless runners, and hunt their prey by chasing them. Cats, on the other hand, hunt by stalking and pouncing.

Like most cats, wildcats usually hunt at night. When a wildcat finds suitable prey, it crouches low and moves slowly and silently towards it. Every so often the wildcat pauses to scent the air and listen for sounds.

Wildcats are not quite the same as the domestic cats we keep as pets. When they are threatened, domestic cats arch their backs, but a wildcat will crouch on its back legs, bare its teeth, and hiss.

When it gets as close as it can, it pounces. With larger prey, such as rabbits, the wildcat rushes at its victim, grapples it to the ground, and kills with a bite to the back of the neck. With smaller prey, such as mice, the cat leaps high into the air and smashes down on the victim from above.

Mating and young

Like most other cats, adult wildcats live alone. Each female lives in a **territory** that is big enough for her to find prey all year round. Males have much larger territories that overlap those of several females. Each cat marks its territory by leaving **scent marks**.

Females are able to **mate** only at certain times, when they are **in season**. At these times males seek out females and try to mate with them. Kittens are born about nine weeks after a successful mating.

Besides rabbits and **rodents**, wildcats also catch birds, fish, frogs, snakes, lizards, and even insects. This one has caught a mole.

As with all cats, the kittens are helpless when they are born, and their eyes are closed. Their eyes open after about two weeks. At this point their eyes are bright blue, but they turn yellow-green as the kittens grow. At about five months of age, the kittens become independent, although they are not able to mate until they are nine to twelve months old.

Female wildcats bring up their kittens on their own, although the male may bring food when the kittens are young.

Other wildcats

It is a winter evening in the mountains of the Gobi Desert. The ground is covered in snow, and it is freezing cold. A grey cat with long fur is crouched motionless, listening carefully. It can hear the faint sounds of a **pika** tunnelling through the snow. After a few moments the cat pounces, breaking through the roof of the snow tunnel to land on the pika.

Pallas's cat, which lives in the **steppes** and mountains of central Asia, is one of several relatives of the wildcat. Wildcat relatives live in a wide range of **habitats**, from the mountains of central Asia to the sands of the Sahara.

Sand cat

The sand cat is a small cat, 40 to 57 centimetres (16 to 22 inches) long. It lives in the hot, sandy deserts of north Africa and south-west Asia. In the heat of the day, the sand cat shelters in a burrow, coming out to hunt at night. It relies mainly on its highly sensitive hearing to find the burrows of **rodents**, such as gerbils. Sand cats also hunt small poisonous snakes. The cat stuns the snake with lightning blows to the head, then bites the back of its neck.

Kittens are born in an underground den about two months after mating. The kittens are tiny, weighing only about 40 grams (1.5 ounces) at birth.

The sand cat does not need to drink. It can get all the liquid it needs from its prey.

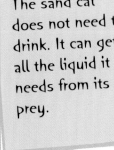

Jungle cats live across the warm southern parts of Asia, from the Middle East to Vietnam.

Black-footed cat

Black-footed cats get their name because the undersides of their feet are black. They are the smallest of all cats, with the very largest males growing to only 50 centimetres (20 inches). They live in dry, open areas in southern Africa.

During the day black-footed cats shelter in burrows they have taken over from other animals, or in old termite mounds. At night they hunt prey, such as ground squirrels, birds, and reptiles. Black-footed cats produce one to three kittens. The kittens develop very quickly – they can walk at two weeks of age, and can run well by six weeks.

Jungle cat

Jungle cats are quite large wildcats, between 50 and 75 centimetres (20 to 30 inches) in length. They live across the warm southern parts of Asia, from the Middle East to Vietnam. Although they do live in forests, jungle cats are also found in more open areas, usually near water. Jungle cats often hunt in water, as well as living by it. They catch fish and other water creatures in shallow water, and will sometimes dive to chase after their prey.

Jungle cats often live near human settlements, where they often feed on chickens. They also live on farmland, especially where it is irrigated.

Ocelot and margay

In an American zoo, two margays live in a large compound with tree branches and ropes stretched across it. The margays play games among the branches and ropes. They leap from a branch to one of the ropes, landing with the rope across their stomach. They somersault around the rope until they are dangling from their back legs, then drop to the ground.

Ocelots and margays are similar-looking cats that live in central and South America. Some ocelots can also be found in the southern USA. They are part of a group of small South American cats that also includes the tiger cat and the pampas cat.

Margays are similar in size to domestic cats, but ocelots are bigger, 67 to 97 centimetres (26 to 38 inches) in length. Ocelots live in a wider range of habitats, including marshlands, grasslands, and all kinds of forest. Margays live only in forested areas.

Ground and tree hunters

Both ocelots and margays are night hunters. The ocelot hunts most of its **prey** on the ground. Its main prey are various kinds of **rodents**, but it also eats lizards, fish, birds, and sometimes the young of larger prey, such as deer and monkeys.

Margays have incredible climbing abilities. They can move around in trees like squirrels or monkeys, leaping from branch to branch and running along the tops of branches or hanging

Ocelots hunt alone, but during the day several ocelots may use the same hiding place to rest. In this picture the male is grooming the female's head in greeting.

A margay's tail is much longer than an ocelot's relative to its body length. This long tail is important for balance when climbing.

underneath them. Margays use their agility to catch a wide range of prey, including climbing rats, squirrels, opossums, capuchin monkeys, and sloths. They also eat small birds and sometimes fruit.

Mating and young

Both ocelots and margays spend their lives in forests or among thick undergrowth, and little is known of their social lives. Ocelots give birth to just one or two kittens in a well-concealed den. Ocelot kittens feed on their mother's milk until they are seven weeks old, when they start to eat meat. Kittens are thought to become independent after about a year.

Margays also produce just one or two kittens. Their dens are often in tree hollows. Margay kittens are comparatively big at birth, and they develop quickly. After five weeks they are eating their first solid food, and they reach adult size after six to eight months.

Hunted for fur

Both ocelots and margays have beautifully patterned coats, and they are hunted for their fur. Ocelot fur is the most valuable, but in some countries there are now laws limiting the hunting of ocelots. This has led to more hunting of margays.

Lynx and bobcat

On a snowy mountainside in Idaho, USA, a bobcat crouches hidden, watching a deer feeding. The deer is far bigger than the bobcat – but the bobcat is hungry. It leaps on the deer, which tries to run with the bobcat clinging to its back. After a few strides the deer stumbles and slows down. The bobcat takes this chance to clamp its jaws round the deer's throat.

With their short tails, **tufted** ears, and **ruff** of fur around the face, lynxes and bobcats look very similar. However, they are different in size and weight, eat different **prey** and mostly live in different habitats.

Lynx

There are two main lynx species. The Canadian lynx lives in northern Canada, while the Eurasian lynx lives in Europe and Asia. Both species prefer forest habitats.

Eurasian lynxes are between 80 and 130 centimetres (31 to 51 inches) long. Their main prey are small deer, such as roe deer and chamois. Where these are less common, lynxes may rely on hares, wild sheep, or large red deer.

Canadian lynxes are smaller and lighter than Eurasian lynxes, and eat smaller prey. They hunt mainly snowshoe hares.

Rarest cat

A third lynx species, the Iberian (Spanish) lynx, is found only in a few parts of Spain. It is probably the world's most **threatened** cat. Although they have been protected since 1974, these lynxes are still illegally shot.

In most places where lynxes live, winters are long and cold. They have extra-large feet that act as "snowshoes", spreading their weight on the snow.

The lives of the Canadian lynx and the snowshoe hare are closely linked. The lynxes depend heavily on the hares for food, and if numbers of snowshoe hares fall, so do the numbers of lynxes.

Like other cats, lynxes rely on stealth to get close to their prey then make a sudden attack. They use their large, clawed feet to grip and pull down prey, then finish them off with a killing bite.

Female lynxes are only **in season** for a short time in early spring. During this time lynxes move outside their normal hunting areas looking for partners. Between one and five cubs are born about ten weeks after **mating**. Cubs remain with their mothers until the following mating season.

Bobcats hunt cottontail rabbits in southern areas, and snowshoe hares in the north, but they can also take large prey several times their own weight.

Bobcats

Bobcats are smaller than lynxes, they have shorter ear tufts, and have smaller feet. They live in a range of habitats from southern Canada to Mexico. Like Canadian lynxes, bobcats hunt mainly rabbits and hares. However, they also eat all kinds of other prey, from birds and rodents to deer.

Bobcats usually mate in early spring, and the female gives birth to between one and four kittens. The kittens stay with their mother for almost a year, learning how to hunt. By the end of their second year they are ready to **breed**.

13

Caracal

A group of doves are drinking at a water hole in southern Africa. In the reeds on the shore a caracal watches, black ears twitching. The caracal crouches then leaps forward, reaching the water's edge in two huge bounds. The birds take flight, but the caracal leaps into the air, and with two lightning swipes of its front paws it brings down two birds.

Caracals are medium-sized cats, 55 to 75 centimetres (22 to 30 inches) long, that live in many parts of Africa and south-west Asia. They are sandy or reddish brown cats with long legs and long ear **tufts** like a lynx. Caracals prefer to live in dry, open habitats, such as grassland and **scrubland**, but they are also found in forest areas.

Agile hunters

Like most cats, caracals usually hunt at night. Their main **prey** are smallish mammals, such as rodents and hares, and birds up to the size of guinea fowl. However, caracals sometimes hunt larger prey such as antelopes and gazelles.

Caracals are strong for their size, aggressive, and very agile. They are famed for their leaping ability, especially when catching birds. Caracals are also good climbers and, like leopards, they will occasionally stow a kill in a tree to keep it safe from other animals.

Caracals can catch birds up to the size of guinea fowl. Like most cats, they are fussy eaters. They pluck the feathers off birds before eating them.

Male and female caracals may spend several days together when they are mating. The male caracal is bigger than the female.

Several mates

Female caracals do not **breed** at just one time of year: they come **in season** at regular times all through the year. When a female is in season she will call and make many **scent marks** to attract males. Often the female will **mate** with two or three males, not just one.

About eleven weeks after successful mating, one to six caracal cubs are born in a cave or burrow. After about a month the cubs are able to leave the den, and by six months they can hunt for themselves.

Caracals among the pigeons

Caracals were once trained by hunters in India and Persia (modern Iran) to chase and bring down deer and game birds. In India they were also placed in a ring with a group of pigeons, and bets were placed on how many of the birds the caracal would knock down in a single strike. This might be the origin of the expression 'to put the cat among the pigeons', which means to say or do something that is likely to cause trouble.

Serval

A serval walks slowly through tall grass, its ears moving like radar dishes as it listens for movement. The serval pauses: it has heard a tiny rustle. The serval moves its head, trying to work out exactly where the sound is coming from. Then it leaps high into the air, coming down feet first on a rat hidden in the grass.

Servals are slightly larger than caracals, 70 to 100 centimetres (28 to 39 inches) long, but they are normally built and weigh much less. They have small heads, long legs, long necks and very large, rounded ears. They are spotted, like cheetahs, but the spots run together into bars on the shoulders and neck. Servals are found in southern Africa, usually in areas close to water where there is plenty of tall grass.

A serval's long neck and long legs give it the height to look over the tall grasses of the wetland areas where it lives.

Hunting by sound

Servals usually hunt at dawn and at dusk. They do not usually hunt larger **prey** as caracals do, but specialize in catching large **rodents**, such as swamp rats. In the long grass of the wetland areas where servals usually live, it is difficult to spot prey, so they rely instead on their excellent hearing. Rodents make many sounds that are too high-pitched for humans to hear, but servals are able to hear these sounds.

Servals also use their leaping abilities to catch birds. Usually they catch the birds between both paws like a goalie making a save. Occasionally servals catch water birds as big as flamingos. Frogs are another favourite food.

A farmer's friend

In some areas servals live on farmland or near human settlements. Very occasionally a serval living near a farm will kill chickens, but more often servals benefit farmers. Rats and other rodents are often pests that eat grain and other farm crops. Servals help to keep the rodent population under control by hunting them. An adult serval eats about 4000 rodents each year.

A new generation

Servals do not **breed** at just one time of year, but most cubs are born in the **wet season**, when there are plenty of rodents to eat. Usually the female has two or three cubs, but occasionally there may be up to five. The cubs begin by drinking only milk, but by four weeks they are beginning to eat some solid food. By five or six months they are eating only meat, and are fully grown within a year.

A serval's eyes and ears stay focused on its prey as it makes a killing pounce.

Puma

In the forests of western Canada, a puma has killed a moose calf. It does not begin to eat immediately – instead it drags the moose to the shelter of some nearby bushes. The calf is over three times the weight of the puma, but the puma moves it easily. After eating as much as it can, the puma covers the moose with leaves and soil, to keep it safe for later.

Pumas (also known as cougars) are found from western Canada to the southernmost tip of South America. They are the biggest cats in North America, but in South America the jaguar is larger. At one time pumas lived right across North America, but today there are very few in the eastern half of the continent.

Pumas are so widespread because they are very adaptable. They can survive in a wide range of habitats, including dry desert areas, **tropical** rainforests, and cold **conifer** forests.

Adaptable night hunters

Pumas hunt mainly in the early evening and before dawn. They are secretive hunters that rely on stealth to catch their **prey**.

Pumas are also adaptable in what they eat. In North America their

An important weapon in the puma's armoury is its tremendous jumping power. It can leap distances of over 12 metres (39 feet).

Pumas can grow to 196 centimetres (77 inches) in length, and can be tawny, reddish, or grey in colour. They are known by many other names – cougars, mountain lions, catamounts, and panthers.

main prey are large animals, such as deer, bighorn sheep, and even young moose. However, in South America, pumas are often competing for food with bigger jaguars. They adapt by eating smaller prey such as large rodents and hares.

Mating and cubs

Pumas do not have a **breeding season**, but in North America most cubs are born in spring and summer. Female pumas usually have two or three cubs. When they are born the cubs have spotted coats. The cubs' eyes are closed at birth, and open at about two weeks of age. By six weeks the cubs can travel with their mother, and by six months they are beginning to hunt for themselves. After six months to a year, the young pumas have lost their spots, but they usually stay with their mother for another year.

Florida panthers

There are no pumas in eastern USA, except in Florida. Here there are small numbers of Florida panthers, a group of pumas that have become isolated from their western relatives. There are fewer than 50 of these pumas left in the wild. To try to save them from **extinction**, some animals have been captured and are being bred in zoos, in the hope that they can be released back into the wild at a later date.

Lion

Four lionesses find a buffalo cow and her calf separated from their herd. The lions drive off the cow and kill the calf. But later the cow comes back, looking for her calf. The lionesses circle the cow warily. Buffalos are difficult **prey** and none of the lionesses wants to attack first. Then a male lion arrives and leaps at the buffalo. The lionesses charge in, too, pulling the buffalo down.

Lions are among the biggest of the big cats. Males are bigger than females – they can be up to 2.5 metres (more than 8 feet) long, and can weigh 240 kilograms (530 pounds).

Lions are one of four cats that can roar – the others are tigers, leopards, and jaguars. The **habitat** they prefer is open woodland, **scrubland**, and **savannah** grassland.

Top hunters

Lions are the most powerful **predators** in Africa, and they regularly hunt larger prey than other cats. They often hunt grazing mammals, such as antelopes, zebra, and wildebeest. When they cannot get these prey they may eat animals as large as buffalo – or as small as insects!

Lions are the only cats that have tufts of hair on the ends of their tails. Males also have large manes of hair on their necks and shoulders, something else not found in other cats.

Lions from the past

Less than 200 years ago there were lions throughout Africa and in several parts of Asia. Today lions are found only in southern and eastern Africa and in a small area (the Gir Forest) in India.

But a few north African lions do still survive in zoos around the world. These Barbary lions, as they are known, are the descendants of "royal" lions that were once kept by the rulers of Morocco.

One of the reasons that lions regularly catch large prey is that, unlike other cats, they live and hunt in groups, called prides.

Life in a pride

At the centre of a pride of lions is a group of closely related lionesses and their young. The lionesses live together in a loose group.

There are also between one and four males in a pride. The males are not related to the females, but they are usually related to each other. They may be brothers or cousins that left their home pride when they became young adults. For a time young adult males live as nomads, with no pride of their own. Once they are fully grown, they try to take over a pride by chasing out the existing males.

Most lion prides have between three and ten adult females, and two to four adult males. Cubs and young lions that are not quite grown can take the numbers up to twenty or more.

21

How lions hunt

In the daytime lions seem to be lazy – most of the time they lie around doing nothing. But at night it is a different story. When night falls the lions set off to patrol their territory and to hunt.

Lions kill different prey in different ways. With antelopes and gazelles, for instance, a lion will kill with a bite to the back of the neck. The lion's long **canine** teeth stab down between the neck bones into the nerves of the spine, paralysing the victim. However, the neck bones of large prey, such as buffalo, are too strong for this approach to work. Instead the lion clamps its jaws around the prey's throat or nose and **suffocates** it.

Like other cats, lions rely on stalking their prey to get close. They then put in a tremendous burst of speed. Over a short distance a lioness can reach speeds of 56 km/h (35 mph).

Lions may hunt together or alone, depending on what prey are available. In the rainy season in the Serengeti plains, for instance, large prey are plentiful. The lionesses hunt in groups of two or more, and one kill is enough to feed the whole pride.

In the dry season the grazing herds move away, and the lions may live on smaller prey, such as warthogs. They may hunt alone, because one animal is not enough to feed everyone.

Many mouths to feed

If a pride lives in an open area, it is usually the lionesses that do most of the hunting. Although they are smaller than males, they are quicker and more agile and therefore better suited for hunting some prey, such as zebras and antelopes. Because they are bigger, males can always muscle in and take a share of any food the lionesses kill.

In more forested areas, animals cannot run away so easily, and male lions often hunt for themselves. Because they are bigger, males can tackle very large prey, such as buffalos, although even a male lion will rarely take on an adult buffalo alone.

What do males do?

The male lions in a pride may seem like lazy bullies, doing no hunting and taking much of the food. However, they do have an important job defending the pride from threats.

One threat to a pride is from other lions. Wandering males are always looking for a chance to take over a pride, or males from a neighbouring pride might try to expand their territory. A group of lionesses could not fend off a threat from male lions.

The male lions in a pride are often involved in fights to keep other males out of their territory.

Hyena trouble

Male lions are also important for defending food from rivals, in particular clans of spotted hyenas. A lioness alone can fend off perhaps four hyenas, but even three or four lionesses may have trouble stopping a large hyena clan from stealing their kill. However, if there is a male lion around, even a large clan is unlikely to steal the food.

Mating and cubs

Lions do not form pairs to **mate** and bring up cubs. Over a period of time all the adult males and females in a pride may mate with each other. Lionesses are only able to mate at certain times, when they are **in season**. Often several females in a pride will be in season at the same time, and will mate with one or more of the pride males.

About 15 weeks after mating, the lion cubs are born. They are tiny and helpless; their eyes do not open until about 10 days after birth. Until they are at least a month old, a lioness keeps her cubs apart from the other lions. After a month she will introduce her cubs to the rest of the pride. If several females have cubs, they join together to form a "**crèche**". The females in the crèche hunt together, and often they will allow cubs other than their own to **suckle**.

Young lions do not become independent until they are one and a half to two years old. At this age males are driven out by the adult males in the pride, and live for a time as wanderers. Females may also be driven out if there is not enough food for them in the pride's territory.

Clans of spotted hyenas are capable of killing large prey, such as zebras. They can also sometimes drive lions away from their kills.

The cubs of several females may live and play together in a "crèche".

What is a roar for?

A pride's territory usually has to be large for them to find enough food all year round. Different pride members may be scattered over a large area, especially at night when they are hunting. One way that lions keep in touch with each other is by roaring. A lion's roar can be heard over eight kilometres (five miles) away, and lions can recognize the roars of other pride members. Lions also roar to announce ownership of a territory or to frighten intruders from other prides.

Tiger

At sunset the tiger gets up, stretches, and sets off to hunt. It pads along **game trails** that run through the forest, senses alert for signs of **prey**. Suddenly the tiger pauses in mid-stride – it has heard the faint sounds of deer feeding. Sinking down on its haunches, the tiger slips into the shadows and begins the slow stalk towards its prey.

Like most cats, tigers usually hunt alone and at night. They are the largest of all cats, and one of the biggest **predators** in the world. The largest type of tiger, the Amur (Siberian) tiger, can be over 3 metres (12 feet) long and weigh 300 kilograms (661 pounds).

From mountains to rainforests

Tigers can survive in a very wide range of **habitats**. They are found in cold northern forests in the far east of Russia, **tropical** rainforests in Sumatra, **mangrove** swamps in Bangladesh, and grasslands in the foothills of the Himalayas. In all places where they live, tigers need tall grasses, bushes, or trees to provide good cover.

Although a tiger's stripy coat really stands out on open or snowy ground, in long grass or among bushes the dark stripes break up the tiger's outline and make it difficult to see.

What tigers eat

Tigers' main prey are deer, wild cattle, and wild pigs. In parts of India the tigers mainly hunt gaur, a kind of wild cattle that weighs 1000 kilograms (2200 pounds) or more. Tigers also sometimes kill and eat other large prey, such as leopards, bears, and even young elephants.

Seriously endangered

During the 20th century the numbers of tigers worldwide plummeted, from perhaps 100,000 at the start of the century to fewer than 7500 at the end. The remaining tigers are split up into several isolated groups, some of which are too small to survive.

There are three main reasons for the drop in tiger numbers. First, huge increases in human populations in southern and eastern Asia have led to the loss of much of the tiger's habitat. Second, loss of habitat has also greatly reduced the numbers of the prey animals that tigers hunt. Third, despite being protected, tigers are still hunted and killed for their bones, which are used in traditional Asian medicines.

Tigers have tremendous explosive power that enables them to overtake prey animals over a short distance. This is why they always live in habitats with plenty of cover – they need to get close to their prey before attacking.

Stalk and ambush

Tigers usually spend the day resting, then go out to hunt at dusk. Generally they actively hunt for food, but they may also lay an ambush, for instance at a waterhole where prey come to drink.

Tigers can eat huge amounts – up to 40 kilos (88 pounds) in one sitting. This is like eating the meat from 172 large burgers!

Only a few tigers remain on the Indonesian island of Sumatra. Tigers on the nearby islands of Bali and Java died out in the 20th century.

If possible, a tiger will approach its prey from behind. When it gets close enough, it bursts from cover and springs on its victim. As with other cats, the tiger bites the back of the neck with smaller prey or bites the throat to suffocate larger prey. Once it has made a kill, a tiger will drag it off to thick undergrowth to eat undisturbed. It cannot eat the whole of a large kill in one sitting, so it hides the rest to eat later.

Water lovers

Domestic cats are famous for not liking water, but tigers are at home in it. In tropical regions tigers spend the hottest part of the day in water, to keep cool. Tigers often hunt close to water, ambushing prey while they are drinking. Sometimes they charge at drinking victims and knock them into the water. Occasionally tigers have been known to kill crocodiles!

Tigers are almost as at home in water as on land. In India, a large population of tigers lives in the Sundarbans region, a huge area of mangrove swamp at the mouth of the River Ganges.

Man-eating tigers

All big cats are dangerous, but tigers have killed more people than any other big cats. Usually they kill people only if they feel threatened, for instance if a farmer tries to defend his livestock from a tiger. Very occasionally a tiger gets a taste for humans and hunts them for food. In the early 20th century one tiger, called the Champawat tiger, is thought to have killed 434 people in northern India and Nepal.

Mating and young

Although they mostly live and hunt alone, tigers are not completely isolated from each other. Female tigers live in fairly small **territories**, which they defend from other females. Males have larger territories that overlap the territories of as many females as possible. Both males and females mark their territories with **scent marks**.

When a female tiger is ready to mate, her scent changes. A male coming across a female's scent mark will be able to tell this. When a male first tries to mate he is often rejected, but after a few days the female usually becomes more friendly and the pair will mate. Two or three cubs are born about fourteen weeks later.

Female tigers usually bring up their cubs alone. The cubs' eyes open after about two weeks, and by eight weeks they are starting to eat meat. After a year they can hunt for themselves, but they do not become completely independent until they are about 18 months old.

Tiger cubs begin to eat meat as well as their mother's milk at about two months of age, but they continue to take some milk until they are six months or so.

Leopard

A female leopard has killed an impala. She begins to eat, but then stops, uneasy. She hears the whooping cries of hyenas. Leaping to her feet, she picks up the impala and carries it towards a nearby fig tree. Before she gets there, two spotted hyenas appear and charge towards her. With a burst of speed the leopard reaches the tree and hauls the impala up into the branches.

Leopards are the most successful of the big cats. There are more leopards than any other big cat, living in a range of **habitats** from the dense rainforests of central Africa and Malaysia to southern parts of the Arabian peninsula.

A varied menu

Like pumas in the Americas, leopards are adaptable predators that will eat almost any animal they can catch. Their diet includes everything from lizards and insects to giraffe calves and wildebeest. Most often, leopards hunt medium-sized grazing animals, such as antelopes, wild goats, and gazelles. These animals are agile and very fast. They can usually escape from a leopard in a chase.

Leopards are masters of stealth. They are probably better than all other cats at getting close to their prey.

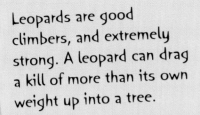

Leopards are good climbers, and extremely strong. A leopard can drag a kill of more than its own weight up into a tree.

To catch such **prey** a leopard needs to get very close – within 20 metres (65 feet) or less before launching an attack. They have to be masters of stealth and secrecy to get this close. Most often they hunt in the dark, when their superb night vision gives them an advantage over their prey.

Silent hunters

Even at night there is usually enough light to see things moving, so a leopard must use every scrap of cover as it approaches its prey. When it is hunting a leopard moves silently, placing each foot with great care as it inches forward. The kill is almost as silent as the approach, with the leopard biting either the back of the neck or clamping down on its victim's throat.

Many rivals

Leopards kill silently because there are often other predators in the area that will steal the leopard's kill if they get a chance. Lions and tigers often drive leopards away from a kill, and they will attack the leopard itself, given the chance. Another serious rival is the spotted hyena. Hyenas are as big as leopards and just as fierce. Their super-sensitive noses can guide them to a kill from over a kilometre (more than half a mile) away.

To escape from these rivals, leopards will often climb a tree. Leopards living in hyena country will often drag their kill up a tree, too.

Separate but overlapping

Adult leopards live and hunt alone, although hunting females often have cubs with them. Adult females defend **territories** large enough to provide food for themselves and their cubs. These territories may overlap at the edges, but the females generally avoid each other.

Male leopards have larger territories, which overlap those of several females. The males avoid the females in their territory most of the time, except when one of them is ready to **mate**. Like other cats, female leopards can only mate and produce young when they are **in season**. When a female comes into season, the smell of her **scent marks** changes, and this may attract a male leopard. She will also call, and seek out a male if she hears him calling.

Leopards survive by being secretive at all times. If a lion spots a leopard, or leopard cubs, it will try to kill them.

Bringing up young

If a male and female leopard mate successfully, the female will produce one to four cubs about three months later. Male leopards almost never help with feeding or looking after cubs – the female must do it all herself. **Suckling** cubs takes a lot of energy, so the female needs to eat more than usual. Once the cubs are a little older, they start to eat meat and she has to hunt for them as well. Females with cubs often have to hunt in daylight as well as at night in order to catch enough food for themselves and their family.

When a female goes hunting, she leaves her cubs hidden away in a den, which could be in a cave or in a thicket. Young cubs stay in the den until their mother gets back, but as the cubs get older they begin to explore the area. Their mother brings back small prey such as rabbits, which she has caught but not killed, for the cubs to practise hunting. By six to eight months of age they are beginning to hunt for themselves.

Leaving home

Once they are about a year old, the mother leopard begins to drive her cubs away with snarls when they approach her. Female cubs may stay in the area and take over part of their mother's territory, but males spend some time as wanderers, getting food wherever they can, until they are old enough and big enough to take over a territory of their own.

Here is a "black panther". Some other cat species also have black forms, especially jaguars.

"Black panthers"

Most leopards are light-coloured with black rosettes (spots). However, a few leopards look totally black. These black leopards were thought at one time to be a different kind of cat – a "black panther". But they do have rosettes, which can be seen if you look closely. In most habitats they are very rare, but in dense forest areas as many as half of the leopards can be black.

Snow leopard

In the foothills of the Himalayas, a group of blue sheep are grazing quietly. Then a snow leopard slinks silently up the slope behind them. The sheep get wind of the leopard and begin to move uphill. They move slowly at first, then start to run. As they reach the top of the slope a second snow leopard leaps from hiding and pulls down one of the sheep.

Snow leopards usually hunt alone, but pairs often hunt together in the **breeding season**. These medium-large cats, up to 130 centimetres (51 inches) long, live in steep, rocky **habitats** in the remote mountains and high plains of central Asia.

High-priced fur

Snow leopards are among the most endangered of all cats. Hunting snow leopards is banned, but they are still killed illegally because people will pay high prices for their fur. A herder who kills a snow leopard can sell the skin for more than a year's wages.

A snow leopard's deep chest and large lungs help it get enough oxygen from the thin mountain air.

Snow leopards can leap even further than pumas. They have been known to jump 15 metres (50 feet). A snow leopard's long tail helps it balance when jumping.

Good in heat or cold

Snow leopards are well adapted to the high places where they live, where the weather is freezing cold in winter and baking hot in summer. The snow leopard's thick fur **insulates** it both from too much heat and from too much cold. The fur that covers the soles of a snow leopard's feet is equally good in snow and on baking hot rocks.

Large prey

Snow leopards mainly hunt large **prey**, such as blue sheep, wild goats, young yaks, and sometimes livestock. Blue sheep (actually a kind of goat) are the main prey for most snow leopards.

Adult snow leopards kill a large prey animal every ten to fifteen days, eating from the kill for up to a week. They tend to hunt in a fairly small area for a period of a week or so, then shift their centre of operations some distance away.

Keeping in touch

Snow leopards range over large areas. To keep in touch they mark commonly used trails with **scent marks** and scrapes. Between January and March, when males and females meet up to **mate**, they make long, wailing calls to communicate.

Snow leopards rarely attack adult yaks – they are too big and heavy. However they do hunt young yaks.

Female snow leopards usually produce two or three cubs. The cubs grow fast, and after only five or six weeks they are making short trips outside the den. However, they stay with their mother for over a year, learning the skills they need to hunt successfully.

Clouded leopard

In a forest in Sumatra, a biologist is setting a leopard trap. Near to a water hole, she places a metal box with an invisible infrared beam to trigger the trap. Inside the metal box is a sophisticated camera. The biologist is using the camera traps to photograph clouded leopards. She uses the information to learn about where clouded leopards travel and hunt.

Clouded leopards are named for the beautiful, cloud-like markings on their fur. Little is known of their behaviour in the wild, because they are extremely secretive animals that are rarely seen. They are medium-sized cats, 60 to 110 centimetres (24 to 43 inches) long, found in the forests of South-east Asia, China, and southern Nepal. Clouded leopards live mainly in dense rainforests, but they are also found in more open forest, **mangrove** swamps, and even grassland.

Agile climbers

The clouded leopard is not a close relative either of the leopard or of the snow leopard. It has short but powerful legs, a long tail for balance, and flexible ankles that help it to climb. Clouded leopards are almost as agile as margays. In captivity, clouded leopards run up and down tree trunks, climb upside-down along horizontal branches, and hang from branches using just their back legs.

In China the clouded leopard is called the mint leopard, because its beautiful patterning is thought to resemble mint leaves.

Disappearing home

Although the hunting of clouded leopards is banned or strictly controlled in most countries, many animals are killed illegally for their beautiful fur. However, a bigger threat to clouded leopards is the rapid disappearance of their forest habitat. In Sumatra, for instance, between 60 and 80 per cent of the lowland forest where clouded leopards live has been cleared to make way for farmland.

Modern sabre-tooth

A clouded leopard's canine teeth are very long. It has been nicknamed "the modern sabre-tooth", because its canines resemble the curved, dagger-like teeth of prehistoric sabre-toothed cats. Scientists have suggested that these long teeth may be designed for killing large prey, or for cutting through the tough skin of wild pigs. However, studies of what clouded leopards eat seem to show that their main prey are monkeys.

Clouded leopards produce between one and four cubs. Cubs have much darker markings than their parents. They develop quickly, opening their eyes after only ten or eleven days, and by five weeks they are quite active. Young clouded leopards are thought to become independent of their mother after about nine months.

The canine teeth of a clouded leopard are very long.

Jaguar

In a quiet river in the Peruvian rainforest, two ripples spread out in a "v" shape across the water. At the point are a pair of nostrils – it is a **caiman** swimming the river. The caiman hauls out on a muddy bank and heads for a small patch of sunlight. Suddenly a large cat explodes out of the undergrowth, lands on the caiman's back, and sinks its teeth into the back of its victim's skull.

Jaguars are the largest cats in the Americas at 112 to 185 centimetres (44 to 73 inches) long, and the third largest in the world after lions and tigers. Jaguars live in rainforests, swampy grassland, and woodlands from northern Mexico to central Argentina.

Telling the difference

A jaguar's coat looks similar to a leopard's, with a pattern of dark, open rings (rosettes). In jaguars there are one to four small spots in the middle of each rosette, whereas in leopards there are no spots.

The name jaguar comes from a South American indian word, yaguara, meaning "an animal that kills its prey with one bound".

Jaguars are excellent climbers. They often climb trees to rest or to keep hidden from prey on the ground.

Powerful jaws

Jaguars are powerfully built cats with a large head and jaws powerful enough to crush bone. They rely on stealth to get as close as possible to their prey. Most cats kill with a bite to the neck or throat. But jaguars, with their extra-powerful jaws, often kill their **prey** by sinking their fangs straight through the skull into the brain, killing them instantly.

All kinds of prey

Jaguars most often hunt large prey, such as peccaries, tapirs, and deer. However, they will eat whatever prey is available in a particular area. In some places, such as the Brazilian Pantanal (a grassland area that floods each year), jaguars come into conflict with ranchers by hunting and eating their cattle.

Wherever they live, jaguars are never far from water. Here they catch fish, **capybara**, and river turtles. Scientists think that the jaguar's powerful jaws originally developed for piercing the shells of turtles and tortoises.

Raising cubs

In many places where jaguars live it is warm all year round, but there is a **wet season** and a **dry season**. Jaguars **breed** at all times of year, but most cubs are born during the wet season, when there is most prey.

Female jaguars give birth to as many as four cubs. They first open their eyes at two weeks, and by about three months they are eating meat and going with their mother on hunts. They stay with their mother until they are about two years old.

Cheetah

On the Serengeti Plains of Africa, a group of Thomson's gazelles are feeding together. One male has wandered a little apart from the herd. A cheetah stalks quietly towards the lone male through the long grasses. When the cheetah is about 100 metres (325 feet) away, the gazelle takes fright and bounds away. Erupting from the grass, the cheetah gives chase. It begins to catch the gazelle, but then suddenly slows down, and the gazelle escapes.

Cheetahs are the sprinters of the cat family. These long-legged cats are the fastest land animals in the world. But cheetahs can only sprint a short distance. Their muscles produce so much energy when they run that after about 500 metres (1640 feet) flat out, they overheat and have to stop.

Cheetahs measure around 123 centimetres (48 inches) in length, which is similar in size to leopards. However they are very different in build, with long legs, a small head, and a slim body. They are found mainly in east and southern Africa.

A different build

Cheetahs are built for speed, and everything else takes second place. A cheetah's long, slim legs and very flexible spine give it an enormous stride. But its slim build makes it less powerful than other big cats.

Cheetahs can reach top speeds of up to 112 km/h (70 mph). They are also incredibly agile at speed, and can match every twist and turn of their prey.

Rivals for food

Although cheetahs are good at catching prey, they do not always get to keep it. Lions, leopards, spotted hyenas, and even the brown hyenas can all drive a cheetah from its kill. Lions also kill cheetah cubs whenever they find them. In the Serengeti Plains, lions and other predators kill as many as 70 per cent of cubs before they become adults.

Cheetahs have a deep chest, to make space for large lungs and a big heart. They also have very wide airways to draw in the maximum amount of air as they run. But to make space for these wide airways, the cheetah's jaws have had to shrink. Over thousands of years, the cheetah's **canine** teeth have become shorter than in other cats, because there is no room for long roots to hold the teeth in place.

Unlike all other cats, cheetahs do not have fully retractable claws. Their protruding claws act like the spikes on a pair of running shoes, giving the cheetah extra grip. Cheetahs also have grooves on their paw pads, which act like the tread on a car tyre. However, as a cheetah's claws are blunted from constant rubbing on the ground, they cannot be used to slash and grapple prey.

Cheetahs often climb rocks, termite mounds, or trees to look out for prey. In this photo it is possible to see the cheetah's **dew claws** (see page 42).

Daytime hunters

Cheetahs hunt by day rather than at night. Their main prey are medium-sized grazers, such as springbok, impala, and Thomson's gazelles. Hunting by day helps avoid competition with the lions and leopards that hunt similar prey by night.

Like other cats, cheetahs stalk their prey, getting as close as they can without being detected. Once it is close enough, the cheetah bursts from cover and begins to run. It has tremendous acceleration, and may catch its prey in this first rush.

As in many other cat species, cheetah mothers catch small prey and then release them so that their cubs can practise hunting.

Giving chase

If the prey escapes the first attack, the cheetah continues the chase. For short distances it can run faster than any of its prey, but it has to get close quickly.

On the inside of their front legs, cheetahs have sharp hooked claws known as dew claws. As it catches up with its victim, a cheetah hooks a dew claw around one of the animal's back legs and trips it up. The cheetah then goes for the prey's throat and kills with a suffocating bite.

An adult cheetah is successful in about half of its hunts. This is a high success rate compared to other **predators**.

Male coalitions

Female cheetahs live alone, but males sometimes live together in "coalitions" of two or three. As with other cats, the males live in **territories**, which they defend against rival males. Female cheetahs sometimes have territories, too, but on the Serengeti, they are nomadic, following the herds of Thomson's gazelles as they travel across the plains. When the gazelle herds pass through the territories of male cheetahs, males and females get together and **mate**.

Mating and young

If mating is successful, a female cheetah will give birth about three months later. Cheetahs produce as many as eight cubs in one litter. The cubs develop quickly, and by the age of six or seven weeks, they can follow their mother on the hunt. This is important, because the mother has to follow the herds if she is to feed herself and her cubs.

As they grow and develop, cubs learn hunting skills. At around eighteen months of age, they are skilled enough to become independent of their mother. The cubs usually hunt together as a group for another six months, until the females are fully adult and ready to mate. Then the females leave, but the males stay together.

Like all cats, cheetahs have a scent gland under their tail, which they use when **scent marking**.

Classification chart

Scientists classify living things (sort them into groups) by comparing their characteristics (their similarities and differences). A **species** is a group of animals or plants that are all similar and can breed together to produce young. Similar species are put together in a larger group called a genus (plural genera). Similar genera are grouped into **families**, and so on through bigger and bigger groupings – classes, orders, phyla, and kingdoms. Plants and animals are the two major kingdoms.

Cats make up the family Felidae, which is part of the Carnivore order (Carnivora). Carnivores are mammals – they belong to the **class** Mammalia.

There are 37 different cat species in 4 genera. Some scientists divide the small cats (genus Felis) into 11 different genera. These are given in brackets below.

Scientific name	Common name
Panthera leo	lion
Panthera tigris	tiger
Panthera pardus	leopard
Panthera onca	jaguar
Panthera uncia	snow leopard
Neofelis nebulosa	clouded leopard
Acinonyx jubatus	cheetah
Felis silvestris	wildcat
Felis chaus	jungle cat
Felis (Otocolobus) manul	Pallas's cat
Felis margarita	sand cat
Felis nigripes	black-footed cat
Felis bieti	Chinese desert cat
Felis (Leopardus) pardalis	ocelot
Felis (Leopardus) tigrinus	tiger cat
Felis (Leopardus) wiedii	margay
Felis (Oreailurus) jacobita	mountain cat
Felis (Oncifelis) guigna	kodkod
Felis (Oncifelis) geoffroyi	Geoffrey's cat
Felis (Oncifelis) colocolo	pampas cat
Pelis (Catopuma) badia	bay cat

Scientific name	Common name
Felis (Catopuma) temmincki	Asiatic golden cat
Felis (Caracal) caracal	caracal
Felis (Profelis) aurata	African golden cat
Felis (Lynx) lynx	Eurasian lynx
Felis (Lynx) canadensis	Canadian lynx
Felis (Lynx) pardina	Iberian lynx
Felis (Lynx) rufus	bobcat
Felis (Pardofelis) marmorata	marbled cat
Felis (Prionailurus) bengalensis	leopard cat
Felis (Prionailurus) iriomotensis	Iriomote cat
Felis (Prionailurus) planiceps	flat-headed cat
Felis (Prionailurus) viverrinus	fishing cat
Felis (Puma) concolor	puma
Felis (Herpailurus) yagouaroundi	jaguarundi
Felis (Leptailurus) serval	serval
Felis (Prionailurus) rubiginosus	rusty-spotted cat

Where cats live

This map shows where some of the cats in this book live.

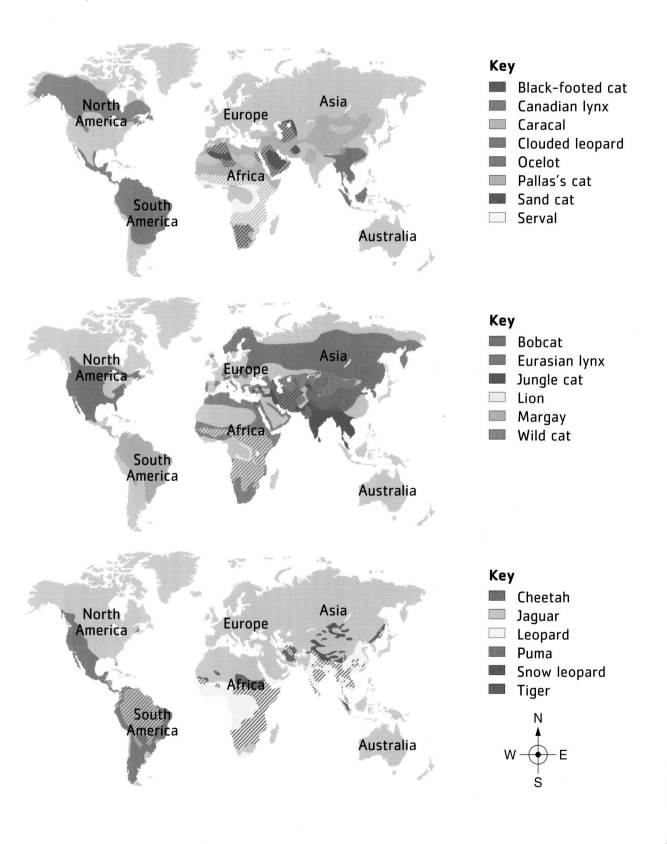

Key

- Black-footed cat
- Canadian lynx
- Caracal
- Clouded leopard
- Ocelot
- Pallas's cat
- Sand cat
- Serval

Key

- Bobcat
- Eurasian lynx
- Jungle cat
- Lion
- Margay
- Wild cat

Key

- Cheetah
- Jaguar
- Leopard
- Puma
- Snow leopard
- Tiger

North America
Europe
Asia
Africa
South America
Australia

N
W E
S

Glossary

breed when animals breed they mate and produce young

breeding season time of year when a group of animals mate

canines long, dagger-like teeth found in the front of a Carnivore's mouth

carnassials shearing (cutting) teeth found in the back of the mouth of all Carnivores

class group of closely related families of living things.

conifer tree such as a pine, fir or spruce, which has needle-like leaves and produces seeds in cones

crèche nursery where babies and young children or animals are cared for

dry season in warm climates there are often two seasons: a wet season with heavy rains and a dry season with little or no rain

extinction when a whole species of living things dies out

family group of closely related genera

game trail track formed by animals travelling regularly along a particular route

habitat the place where an animal lives

in season time when a female cat, or other animal, is ready to mate

insulate to stop heat passing through

mangroves trees found only in warm climates that grow in very wet, swampy ground

mating when a male and a female animal come together to produce young

muzzle the front part of the head of a cat or dog

predator animal that hunts and eats other animals

prey animals that are hunted by predators

pupil the dark spot in the centre of the eye that lets in light

retract to draw in

rodents mammals with sharp, gnawing front teeth, such as rats, mice, and squirrels

ruff ring of longer hair or feathers around the neck

savannah grassland with scattered bushes and trees

scent marking marking a territory with urine or droppings

scrubland area of low, evergreen, leathery-leaved shrubs, many of which are also aromatic (strong-smelling)

species group of animals that are similar and can breed together to produce healthy offspring.

steppes large grassland areas in Russia and central Asia.

suckle to provide mother's milk from the breast

suffocate to cut off an animal's air supply

territory area that an animal lives and hunts in, which it defends from other animals of the same species and sex

threatened in danger of becoming extinct

tropics/tropical lands close to the Equator, where the weather is warm all year

tufted having tufts of longer fur

wet season in warm climates there are often two seasons: a wet season with heavy rains and a dry season with little or no rain

Further information

Books

Big Cat Diary: Leopard, Jonathan and Angela Scott (Collins, 2003).
Big Cat Diary: Lion, Jonathan and Angela Scott (Collins, 2003).
Big Cat Diary: Cheetah, Jonathan and Angela Scott (Collins, 2004).
Written in conjunction with the BBC television Big Cat Diary programmes, each of these books gives an intimate and detailed portrait of one of the three African big cats.

Animals Under Threat: Bengal Tiger, Richard and Louise Spilsbury (Heinemann Library, 2004).
A book that highlights the threats faced by this endangered species.

Organizations and websites

http://lynx.uio.no/catfolk/
The Cat Specialist Group of the IUCN (World Conservation Union). A group of leading scientists researching wild cat species and how to conserve them. The website includes detailed information on all 36 wild cats and a newsletter, Cat News.

http://dspace.dial.pipex.com/agarman/bco/ver4.htm
An interesting and comprehensive website on wild cats, both big and small.

http://nationalzoo.si.edu/Animals/GreatCats/
Smithsonian National Zoological Park. This website from the USA's most important zoo includes cat facts, a photo gallery, and a tiger webcam.

www.bbc.co.uk/nature/programmes/tv/bcd/
Big Cat Diary. Website of the BBC television series. It includes background information on the big cats featured in the programmes and short video clips.

Index

Titles in the *Wild Predators!* series include:

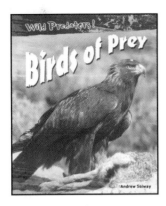

Hardback   0431189927

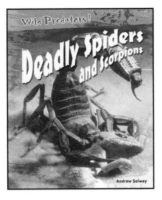

Hardback   0431189943

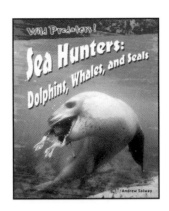

Hardback   0431190070

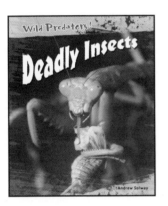

Hardback   0431190038

Hardback   0431190054

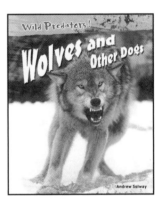

Hardback   0431189951

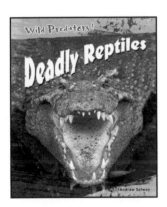

Hardback   0431190046

Hardback   0431190062

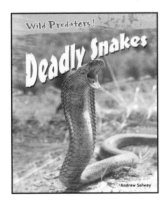

Hardback   0431189935

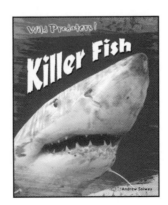

Hardback   0431189919

Find out about the other titles in this series on our website www.heinemann.co.uk/library